Foundation

THIS BOOK WAS DONATED BY
The Sacramento Public Library Foundation
Books and Materials Endowment

The Sacramento Public Library gratefully acknowledges this
contribution to support and improve Library services in the community.

SACRAMENTO PUBLIC LIBRARY

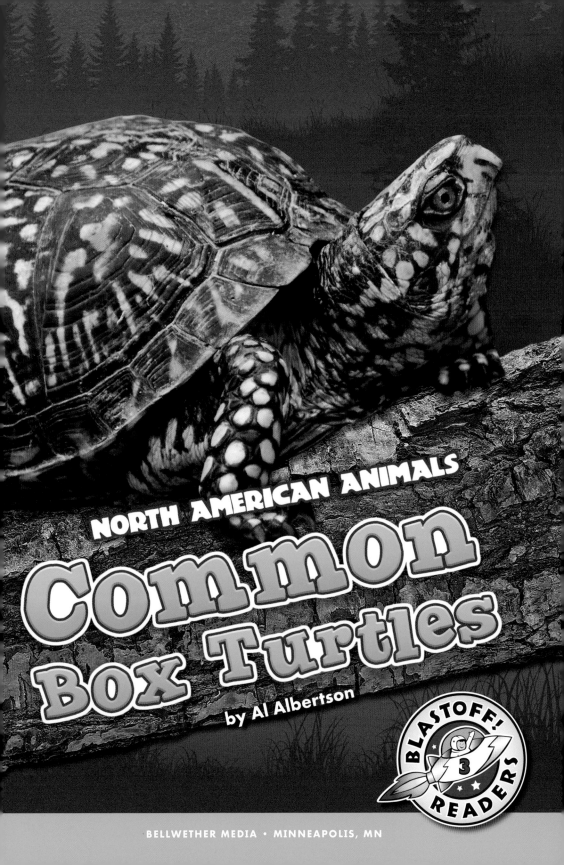

NORTH AMERICAN ANIMALS

Common Box Turtles

by Al Albertson

BELLWETHER MEDIA • MINNEAPOLIS, MN

Note to Librarians, Teachers, and Parents:

Blastoff! Readers are carefully developed by literacy experts and combine standards-based content with developmentally appropriate text.

Level 1 provides the most support through repetition of high-frequency words, light text, predictable sentence patterns, and strong visual support.

Level 2 offers early readers a bit more challenge through varied simple sentences, increased text load, and less repetition of high-frequency words.

Level 3 advances early-fluent readers toward fluency through increased text and concept load, less reliance on visuals, longer sentences, and more literary language.

Level 4 builds reading stamina by providing more text per page, increased use of punctuation, greater variation in sentence patterns, and increasingly challenging vocabulary.

Level 5 encourages children to move from "learning to read" to "reading to learn" by providing even more text, varied writing styles, and less familiar topics.

Whichever book is right for your reader, Blastoff! Readers are the perfect books to build confidence and encourage a love of reading that will last a lifetime!

This edition first published in 2020 by Bellwether Media, Inc.

No part of this publication may be reproduced in whole or in part without written permission of the publisher. For information regarding permission, write to Bellwether Media, Inc., Attention: Permissions Department, 6012 Blue Circle Drive, Minnetonka, MN 55343.

Library of Congress Cataloging-in-Publication Data

Names: Albertson, Al, author.
Title: Common Box Turtles / by Al Albertson.
Description: Minneapolis, MN : Bellwether Media, Inc., [2020] | Series:
   Blastoff! Readers. North American Animals | Audience: Age 5-8. | Audience:
   K to Grade 3. | Includes bibliographical references and index.
Identifiers: LCCN 2018050768 (print) | LCCN 2018051500 (ebook) | ISBN
   9781618915221 (ebook) | ISBN 9781626179820 (hardcover : alk. paper)
Subjects: LCSH: Box turtle–Juvenile literature.
Classification: LCC QL666.C547 (ebook) | LCC QL666.C547 A43 2020 (print) | DDC 597.92–dc23
LC record available at https://lccn.loc.gov/2018050768

Editor: Kate Moening   Designer: Laura Sowers

Printed in the United States of America, North Mankato, MN.

Table of Contents

What Are Common Box Turtles?

Common box turtles are **reptiles**. They are found in the eastern United States and northeastern Mexico.

N W E S

Extinct

Extinct in the Wild

Critically Endangered

Endangered

Vulnerable

Near Threatened

Least Concern

common box turtle =

conservation status: vulnerable

Common box turtles live in forests and fields near water. Many live to be more than 100 years old!

Common box turtles have dark shells shaped like **domes**. The shells are colored with orange or yellow markings.

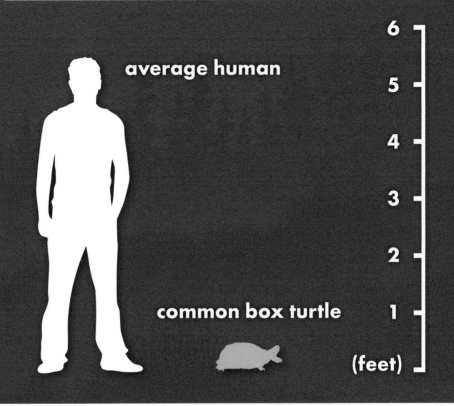

Size of a Common Box Turtle

average human

common box turtle

6 —
5 —
4 —
3 —
2 —
1 —
(feet)

These turtles are usually about 4 to 6 inches (10 to 15 centimeters) long.

webbing

Common box turtles have **webbed feet** for swimming.

dome-shaped shell

orange or yellow markings

claws

They also have sharp claws. These help the turtles climb logs and sandy banks!

Common box turtles are
most active during the summer.
They do not like weather
that is too hot or too cold.

In the north, the turtles **hibernate** during the winter. They hide in empty **burrows** or under the roots of big trees.

burrow

Common box turtles are **omnivores**. Young common box turtles eat mostly meat. They swim to catch small fish and slugs.

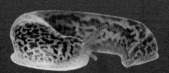

earthworms

leopard slugs

wild strawberries

blackberries

Adults eat mostly plants.
They **forage** for berries
and flowers.

Hard to Hunt

Few **predators** can eat adult common box turtles. These turtles can pull their heads and legs into their shells.

They close the top and bottom parts of their shells. Their shells are almost impossible to open!

The youngest common
box turtles are very small.
Sometimes they are as
small as a penny!

American crows

raccoons

cottonmouths

brown bats

Their shells are soft. They cannot **defend** themselves. Young turtles often become **prey** for bigger animals.

In the spring and summer, female common box turtles dig nests in sandy soil. They lay up to 11 small eggs in the nest.

Then, the mother covers the eggs with soil. She leaves the babies to grow.

nest

hatchling

In about three months, **hatchlings** come out of the eggs. They head for water to start a long life!

Baby Facts

Name for babies:	hatchlings
Number of eggs laid:	up to 11 eggs
Time spent inside egg:	about 3 months
Time spent with mom:	1 day

Glossary

burrows—holes or tunnels that some animals dig for homes

defend—to keep safe

domes—structures with a rounded top and circular base; a dome looks like half of a ball.

forage—to go out in search of food

hatchlings—baby common box turtles

hibernate—to spend the winter sleeping or resting

omnivores—animals that eat both plants and animals

predators—animals that hunt other animals for food

prey—animals that are hunted by other animals for food

reptiles—cold-blooded animals that have backbones and lay eggs

webbed feet—feet with skin that connects the toes

To Learn More

AT THE LIBRARY

Gladstone, James. *Turtle Pond.* Toronto, Ont.:
Groundwood Books, 2018.

Hansen, Grace. *Freshwater Biome.* Minneapolis,
Minn.: Abdo Kids, 2017.

Sabelko, Rebecca. *Common Snapping Turtles.*
Minneapolis, Minn.: Bellwether Media, Inc., 2019.

ON THE WEB

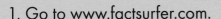

FACTSURFER

Factsurfer.com gives you
a safe, fun way to find
more information.

1. Go to www.factsurfer.com.

2. Enter "common box turtles" into the search box
   and click 🔍.

3. Select your book cover to see a list
   of related web sites.

Index

The images in this book are reproduced through the courtesy of: dora modley-paris, front cover; William Wise, pp. 4-5; Anthony Cedrone, pp. 6-7, 9 (top left, top right); Ivan Kuzmin/ imageBROKER/ agefotostock, pp. 8-9; Studio DMM Photography, Designs & Art, p. 9 (top middle, middle); By Christian Puntorno, p. 10; Aaron Bastin/ Alamy, p. 11; Joe Blossom/ Alamy, pp. 12-13; kzww, p. 13 (top left); Meister Photos, p. 13 (top right); EM Arts, p. 13 (bottom left); grey_and, p. 13 (bottom right); stanley45, pp. 14-15; Sean Wandzilak, p. 15; Byron Jorjorian/ Alamy, p. 16; K Quinn Ferris, p. 16 (top left); Eric Isselee, p. 16 (top right); IsaacSzabo, p. 16 (bottom left); Kirsanov Valeriy Vladimirovich, p. 16 (bottom right); Ariel Bravy, pp. 18-19; NaturePL, pp. 19, 20-21; Robert Hamilton/ Alamy, p. 21 (top); valzan, p. 21 (bottom).